Analog Synthesis

Analog Synthesis

Poems by

Christopher Fried

© 2025 Christopher Fried. All rights reserved.
This material may not be reproduced in any form, published,
reprinted, recorded, performed, broadcast,
rewritten, or redistributed without
the explicit permission of Christopher Fried.
All such actions are strictly prohibited by law.

Cover design by Shay Culligan
Cover image by Derrick Brooks
Author photo by Christopher Fried

ISBN: 978-1-63980-731-4
Library of Congress Control Number: 2025935312

Kelsay Books
502 South 1040 East, A-119
American Fork, Utah 84003
Kelsaybooks.com

*for those who blew into NES cartridges
and adjusted the tracking on VHS tapes*

Acknowledgments

The author thanks the editors of the following journals and webzines in which these poems, sometimes in different versions, first appeared:

Cosmic Daffodil Journal: "More Android Than Androids"
Grand Little Things: "Escape (No One Said the Coming Dystopia Would Be So Tedious)," "Sidekicks and Dames"
Lothlorien Poetry Journal: "Culture Warrior," "Life Turns Tragic for Mr. Charles Beaumont"
The Lyric: "Valens' Dreams at Adrianople"
New English Review: "Crocodiles and Tigers," "Florida Fire Ant Tide," "Golden Streets," "History's Wild Dance (Re-Reading *Blood Meridian*)," "Imagination Questing," "James City County Mall Memorial," "John Self(less)," "Nagel Ladies"
The Pennsylvania Review: "The Bookstore Jazz Quartet," "Croquet as Ritual," "The Day Death Walked into a Restaurant," "George Schuyler at the *Pittsburgh Courier,* 1964," "How the Stars Flicker Under Eyes (Cowboy Strode)"
The Piker Press: "Adventure Remains," "Hollywood's Last Cowboy," "Portals," "The Prophet's Voice (In Memoriam Dave Smith, 1950–2022)," "Video Armageddon"
The Raven Review: "Retina of the Mind's Eye"
The Road Not Taken: A Journal of Formal Poetry: "Hear the Kaiju Roar (Akira Ifukube)," "The Last Roman of the South (Allen Tate)"
Shot Glass Journal: "Mr. Montgomery, Keep Movin'," "Small-Town Lights"
Snakeskin Poetry Webzine: "Pop Pulp (Spillane)," "Scene at a Beach: Hyperion's Woman"
The Society of Classical Poets: "Bright Light, Some City (After Edward Hopper's *Morning Sun*)," "Croquet as Ritual," "Flame Parrots at the Monticello Gardens," "Indian Hill Cemetery, 1953" (as "Campaign of 1940–1952")

Sparks of Calliope: "Longstreet's Postbellum Letters," "Old Devil," "Sundown at Kenyon College," "To the Nation's Credit"
Star*Line: "What Goes There?"
The Storyteller: "Red Warren's Red Loam"
WestWard Quarterly: "Back to Reality After Space-Time Conundrums," "Son and Father"

Grateful acknowledgment is made to the following editors and writers who provided feedback and appreciation for these poems: C.B. Anderson, Madisen Bellon, Randal A. Burd Jr., Vince Gotera, Mary-Jane Grandinetti, Kathryn Jacobs, Strider Marcus Jones, Patrick Key, Richard Leonard, the late Shirley Anne Leonard, Evan Mantyk, Jean Mellichamp Melliken, Sand Pilarski, Joseph Salemi, E.M. Schorb, George Simmers, Harvey Stanbrough, and Rachel Strickland.

Thanks to all the associates, friends and family over the years: Robin Block (along with my fellow advisors for *In Search of Tomorrow (2022)*), Sean Charles, Gwendolyn Brown Consentino, Dominic Curley, Mario Curley, Andrew Donahue, Brandon Evans, Christie Foreman, Joshua Fried, Kelci Haag, Glen Hadley Jr., J.J. Harris, Walter Harris, Priyanka Henriquez, Canaan Hill, Tyler Hummel, Sarah Sloan Iracane, Amber Jennings, Amanda Lang, Tabitha Myers Lilly, Nicol Jean Law, Jared Loer, Schuyler Lolly, Joe Luppino-Esposito, Jason Mixon, Jade Myers, Alex Phillips, Ryan Robledo, Devon Rossler, Chris Skeens, Jon Skeens, Nicholas Smith, Ten (along with my fellow writers at *NewRetroWave*), Dominic Wallis, Christia Webb, Brent Wilburn, and others that I failed to mention. You are the last analog generation!

Thanks to my parents: Jeremy and Elizabeth Fried.

Appreciation to the various synthwave artists that stay retro: Arcade Summer, Baldocaster, Beckett, Betamaxx, CJ Burnett, d.notive, DJ Ten, Dana Jean Phoenix, Droid Bishop, Highway Superstar, Hill Valley Hero, Ian Alex Mac, Interruptor, Jason Mysteria, Jessy Mach, Le Cassette, Let's Talk, Manhatten, Max Cruise, Mega Drive, Michael Weber, MicroMatScenes, The Midnight, Mitch Murder, OGRE Sound, OSC, Perturbator, Phaserland, Robert Parker, Ron Cannon, SelloRekt / LA Dreams, SURGE, TOMMY '86, Turbo Knight, VIDEO8, and Waveshaper, among the other synth enthusiasts that I haven't named.

Contents

I. Retro Speculative

Wave Cycles	17
Imagination Questing	22
Sidekicks and Dames	23
Son and Father	24
Croquet as Ritual	25
History's Wild Dance (Re-Reading *Blood Meridian*)	27
Flame Parrots at the Monticello Gardens	28
Scene at a Beach: Hyperion's Woman	29
Golden Streets	30
ISOT Premiere at Harmony Gold Theater	31
Second Inauguration	33
Back to Reality After Space-Time Conundrums	34
More Android Than Androids	35
What Goes There?	36
Retina of the Mind's Eye	37
Hidden	38
Mutating Passion	39
Escape (No One Said the Coming Dystopia Would Be So Tedious)	40
John Self(less)	41
The Prophet's Voice (In Memoriam Dave Smith, 1950–2022)	42
Portals	43
Silver Screen Maestro	44
McDonald's and Me	46
Small-Town Lights	47
The Bookstore Jazz Quartet	48
The Day Death Walked into a Restaurant	49
Nagel Ladies	50

Hollywood's Last Cowboy	51
Adventure Remains	52
Avian Equation	53
The Byrd (Annus Horribilis)	54
Video Armageddon	56
Not So Similar	57
Home Sweet Home	58
Florida Fire Ant Tide	59
Crocodiles and Tigers	60
James County Mall Memorial	61
Popcorn	62

II. Iconoclasts

Iconoclast	65
Valens' Dreams at Adrianople	66
Old Devil	67
Bright Light, Some City (After Edward Hopper's *Morning Sun*)	68
To the Nation's Credit	70
Indian Hill Cemetery, 1953	71
George Schuyler and the *Pittsburgh Courier,* 1964	72
Power Battle	73
Culture Warrior	74
Life Turns Tragic for Mr. Charles Beaumont	75
How the Stars Flicker Under Eyes (Cowboy Strode)	76
Mr. Montgomery, Keep Movin'	77
Eyes Open	78
Longstreet's Postbellum Letters	79
Red Warren's Red Loam	80

The Last Roman of the South (Allen Tate)	81
Hear the *Kaiju* Roar (Akira Ifukube)	82
Pop Pulp (Spillane)	83
Sundown at Kenyon College	84
Notes	87

I. Retro Speculative

Wave Cycles

It's like the "Stranger Things" of music.
—Ben Umanov

    I. Outrun

Go back to 1986,
and who'd believe the legacy
of this split genre was once bricked
by a joyride game in 3D.

This year, say it's repetitive,
the sequences and machine beats
are but old hat, but it'll give
excitement even on repeat.

    II. Business

Those snobbish won't hold it romantic
to sit back in your chair, e-mailing
one client while the others, frantic
at the last-minute, phone their failings.

The wheeler-dealers hustling down
the office hall don't mean to bump
against—it's their adult playground,
but not another pump-and-dump.

    III. Sweat

Remember Simmons and his band
of smiling women dancing, hands
held high above each other's heads,
with no care how it looked white bread.

Years may have made it parody,
the joyous ladies dance no longer
where twists and turns were judgment-free,
but dormant sleeps their spirit's hunger.

IV. Dream

Whenever I stop, meditate
about the ocean, Debussy's
La Mer replays, reactivates
a scene played out as fantasy.

Sand only tickles laid-out feet
while rolling waves touch in repeat.
What's real are scyphozoan stings
and roomy women in G-strings.

V. Mall

Astride the escalator, crowds
ascend to new displays of joy.
Sounds of teens will echo loud,
while their parents buy new toys.

Aromas sweet and salty sift
through the chilled, circulating air,
and while some march, more others drift
to the once famous voice and stare.

VI. Pop

Sounds denigrated forty years
ago as bubblegum and floss
pull from the youth nostalgic tears
for what they never lived but lost.

Who could believe there's innocence
in undertones that made us wince.
Alone the melancholy croon
while others speak in Auto-Tune.

VII. Chill

We're not about braving the mall's
congestion. Crowds would wreck our nerves,
and as we watch the leaves of fall,
the thought of traffic slows our verve.

It's not as busy now as when
mall management lists new events
for summertime, but we still feel
the need to rest despite fall deals.

VIII. Vapor

The glory days were swept aside
when technology advanced
and we logged in for this new ride.
The mall contracted its expanse.

And still we think of what once was:
the sterile air, the Musak droning
in the background—it gives some pause
as either chosen brings some groaning.

   IX. Horror

Who'd guess that trashed b-movie schlock
would have more memory than praised
Best Pictures with forgotten walks
on the red carpet and scenes replayed

of award-winning monologues.
It may be common, but the viewers
know what they crave, and it's not slogs
through "real-life" drama. It's the sewers.

   X. Dark

No matter whether blade or laser,
the atmosphere is still the same:
You're fleeing the slash-happy razor
as you scream out, but it's no game.

Dystopia arrives as varied
imagination wrought, unburied,
alive, but captive in lit spires,
while wyverns screech amidst their pyres.

XI. Cyber

The prophets of the future shrank
back when they touched what had come true
as they'd been called critics and cranks.
Today they sing the Voight-Kampff blues.

Online connection isn't what
it was supposed to be. Confused
the man and android become. Gut
out information for misuse.

XII. Space

Beyond the devastating crash
of '86, we vision more
than earth despite the snide backlash
against the nifty-named Star Wars.

Flight as the citizen's domain,
(Who could imagine when the shuttle
came crashing down as burning rain?),
returns as the late Ron's rebuttal.

Imagination Questing

More than a boy's adventure, going back
beyond these cynical times, those days pointed
to no end of rough play, staged cul-de-sac-
placed action scenes rehearsed, and whips anointed
with blood by accident. Feigned punches didn't
connect, but to tense mothers there's bare dangers
and rules not always said, with jests forbidden
by parents shushing down raised party clangor.

At bedtime, tired but keen, my father voiced
known Bible stories: welcome tales of swords,
sweet frankincense, and how Israel rejoiced—
the Ark revealed the presence of the Lord!

And though the Ark is gone, still stands the credence
that mocked joys bring angelic intercedence.

Sidekicks and Dames

Neglected and disowned works place among
the serious to view under new eyes,
for years can rectify bias and lies
bandied about as critics' common song.

Is there no teaching of film history?
And do the scoffers know of *Gunga Din?*
Life must be safe, and stereotypes are sins.
So, anything goes? No? We're truly free!

The damsel isn't errant as you felt,
and Mr. Round is a fine child performer.
These thoughts may shock as special effects melts:
I'm just a simple fan, no social reformer,
and I'll embrace the tomatoes you pelt
for your pretense makes you the best performer.

Son and Father

We aim to be as different from our fathers
when we're riled teens; we're questers of what's novel,
and our youth will transport us through all bothers.

The father's mind, in contrast, is a hovel,
unknowing, unconcerned with what a son
enjoys, as old as excavated fossils.

We age and realize in the long run
that our split quests weren't unalike,
especially if our crusade seems won,

and even not, (this trip on life's turnpike
exacts expensive tolls), we glory in
what could be done and try to yield Christlike.

Reality is time makes us has-beens
without any consent, and penitent
as can be, contra father, we'll soon sin.

Our image shifts, and we misrepresent
the past for which we wish and words we meant.

Croquet as Ritual

The season shifts to rest as frost
begins to coat the patterned lawn.
The tangent wooden spheres that crossed
such narrow spaces just draw out yawns

from us settling the final game,
we who heard laughter in the spring.
Dressed ritually in white, we frame
the year in terms of mallet swings,

and so, the time comes for an end
to our priesthood of scholar-preps
till swollen winter retreats and mends
the court we served with our footsteps.

We meditate about the reason
each year we continue to ordain
our lives with meaning when the season
of simple lawn games comes again.

Just like a quest for mythic rites,
and just as arcane, the sequence starts
over when evening takes in daylight
later as the fall hours depart.

Some act off one another, eyeing
a pattern through the outlined course:
the hoop, the strike, the ball just lying
for an endgame by some tour de force.

And others join, having the sport
itself as the sole end. With skill
for skill's sake, reverence helps support
set efforts despite the missing will.

We gather as passé gentlemen
within a slight, barbarian age
and speculate about the end
someday, and still, we silence our rage.

History's Wild Dance (Re-Reading *Blood Meridian*)

for Cormac McCarthy (1933–2023)

Not one to hide grotesque realities
despite the human tendency to peek
between the trembling fingers. Moral law
is set against the gnawing history
of blood v. blood and appetite persists.
What's left are obligations as to man.

In '84, the floodgates holding back
a flush of horrors all-too human failed
as the doomed Brileys seized security
and throttled as they had the innocent
five years before, and this, another land,
long after Glanton's gang rode wild with death.

For here, as then, monsters are not a race
as separate but sprung from the seed of Seth.

Flame Parrots at the Monticello Gardens

I admit at one point that flowers
in themselves didn't matter to me.
We could agree there is some power
apportioned to them, as tourists see

with wonder how color and shape
exist beyond the normality
accustomed to. I too would rate
them nice, but hunt for reality

within the bulbs some touched with little
imagination. I felt the heat
of a land unknown within the middle
gardens, and tasted it as sweet

despite the great distance from soil
of that Lone Star state. These transplants
out east are to their essence loyal—
it takes humility to recant

a prior nonchalance to others'
observations, and learn to love
these flowers just as a father and mother
regard your traits as from above.

Scene at a Beach: Hyperion's Woman

Mosquitoes were heavy that year. He took
precautions, shifting concerns while he drank
a glass of bourbon straight, resisting fast
the currents of the afternoon winds. Next,
he nearly drifted to sleep, with the wind lashing
against his hand, but eyes, heavy as lightning,
will lift at times, and what did his drowsing eyes
engage but Mandy tanning, fierce as the sand
falling off between her toes. But he
digressed as her name isn't Mandy. She
just looked like Mandy, strange as that may sound.
Life is mysterious that way sometimes,
but he again returned with random thoughts
and furtive looks. "Look how pneumatic the scene
appears as the sun sinks with subtle slides
into the ocean distance and hot winds
continue lapping up the patterned sweat
formed from the subtle motion of clothed skin!"

He downed the drink and slept with leveled eyes
as myth returned in little moments. "The sun
will touch with longing of hot breaths, but who
cares when the moment brandishes refulgence
like city skylines stripped to neon lights
and a heat ascendant while club drifters dance."

The sand still burns, and the sun drowns when done,
so, woman, sift the rays with a returned kiss
and embrace the marks for the last hours of light
as you turn over in tribute one more time.

Golden Streets

I'd be safe and warm if I was in L.A.
　　　　—"California Dreamin'"

The early morning flight across
　　　　the States was not the worst or awful
at all as turbulence just tossed
　　　　a little, and the food, not offal
that's normally rolled out on trays,
　　　　did much to settle scabrous nerves
left thrilled by this westbound airway
　　　　set course to L.A.'s relaxed verve,
and as I'm cruising steadily
　　　　north to The Moment Hotel, time
of day was stressed, but what's to see
　　　　but homeless tents and scenic grime.
With windows up, it's not that there's
　　　　some smell or any fears that crooks
will violently wake and stare,
　　　　but just this is where my eyes look,
and even the starred Walk of Fame
　　　　won't scintillate as bright as streams
of urination that are aimed
　　　　at tourists on these streets that teem
with manners left to be desired,
　　　　and still youths come, believing stars
can still be found and those admired
　　　　will not be thought of as bizarre.

ISOT Premiere at Harmony Gold Theater

The crowd waits patiently for what
        took years to reach fruition. Time
had felt slowed down when much was shut
        down due to Covid's climb.
We dreamed of science fiction, and during
        those years we had lived it, the real
not being as exciting; boring
        contrasted with the feels
we watchers get when films from youth
        are played once more, and dialogue
we know from memory still soothes.
        Time calls films pedagogues.
Still, here we sit as speeches end,
        which introduces this fan's doc
to all who trekked here to attend
        to take this five-hour block
and smile at a projected screen.
        All lights around the room are dimmed
while we watch scenes we've watched umpteen
        times, though on T.V., trimmed.
As such, tears leak from eyes of these
        who sit in silence, with exception
when a triumphant scene that pleased
        when young provides connection
despite our different ages, varied
        beliefs, or where we travelled from.
There's laughter, screams, and all that's married
        to memories succumbed
to when just film snippets are shown,
        and even these emotions scattered
throughout the room are just a few tones
        when fans of all kinds gather.

The premiere done, those heading home
        know that the past as was will not
return as is, but desires roam
        to loved joys we forgot.

Second Inauguration

Never had winds cut and frost coat the land
as then in January '85,
or at least since the weather records mattered,
and all throughout the nation people huddled
to wait till this cold wave phenomenon
had passed. One hundred twenty-six or more
froze in their beds, the citrus crop collapsed,
and properties became as safe as silk
athwart the gusts, but there's more delight then
despite the peril than now amidst the toys
and trinkets that facilitate our sleep
amongst anxieties.
                    In hushed D.C.
a grand voice sang of simple gifts, parades
were cancelled, and the Gipper retook an oath,
while life itself began again as south
a couple hours or more some child arrived
without much celebration but by few,
a natural son adopted to nice folks.

With newborn hands outstretched to a cold world,
in imitation of the day, he cooed
as sunlight slipped through all the snow and shade.

Back to Reality After Space-Time Conundrums

Time travel doesn't make much sense when you
get down to it despite romancing hope
of seeing what we thought as what was then
or what will be as more than fantasies,
for what becomes of all that has accrued
into the present person?—haunting trope
if there's one single change, all that we were
disintegrates until we're nobody
familiars recognize.
                        "How could McFly
return, with all he did to change things up,
and he still be the same Hill Valley kid?
This flux would shift his personality."

Such are nostalgic musings crossing slopes
of philosophical slants but not true.

More Android Than Androids

When looking back at film predictions
of what the future would entail,
these always visualized empowered
thugs clamping down the speaking few
or bleaker wasteland death depictions,
the follow-up from countervails
as the warheads soar, detonate
above the waiting crowded queues.

Who would've guessed machines would make
us able servants, not by force
or lasers shot by Nexus-Six,
but by wavelengths of lambent blue.

New breakthrough tech is science fiction
grown wildly from once-new email.

What Goes There?

We know this dormant creature braces
and hides in blood and molecules,
then explodes out with twisted faces:
thus, making us estranged, so cruel.

Most times we don't know when this thing
will stir. Tension or fear transforms
our flesh and mind into a thing
grotesque: our hale ideal deformed.

We reach for some connection still
despite the paranoia and masks
we believe others wear to feel.
"And what goes there?" our silence asks.

Retina of the Mind's Eye

Across the home, around the neighborhood,
screens small to large turn off and on. The lights
bleed out the windows as libations poured
as one to new, mysterious idols.

Reality, in turn, becomes confused
as something less than what's viewed. Acolytes,
these surge in simulated fears and bliss
while the new gods with images cajole
the assembly to move to weirder thoughts,
the congregated to become less bored
as simple patterned provocation wanes.

As the screens pulse, they can't resist the pull,
whether sharp LED or megabytes,
and bow their heads in the light of their lords.

Hidden

*Knowing your own darkness is the best method
for dealing with the darknesses of other people.*
—Carl Jung

Submerged beneath an outer shell
        is his truest health
and realities he sinks to tell
        no one and hide from himself.

Some alien emotion gnaws
        him heedless bound to where
he should demur, but he withdraws
        into sought filth and flair.

This cyclic life as citizen
        and family man is so numbing,
but a parasitic slug within
        must be the cause for this slumming.
He breaks society's constraints,
        implodes all vows as nothing,
and says the conscience is what taints,
        and he still hides his blushing.

Is it his worm inside that dashes
        and drags to wrong, the ill-
conceived and worst, the rashes
        of thefts, deceits, and kills?

Perhaps this alien aspect
        is a human feature
that some readily reject
        while he transforms the creature.

Mutating Passion

No change is easy, but this state would be
so unexpected: chance unleashed its spark
to sear these two as one, and turned the lonely
into the loved, one hopes without a price.
Though love still lasts, his curiosity
had killed his test baboon, then stripped him stark
of what he was: the scientist, once homely,
reborn unmanned because of a gene splice.

So now more beast than man, what would he do?
What's her next step? She meditates like Titus
Andronicus mused what is right for ill
unfavored flies. Embracing ceded truth
that what was love decayed into detritus,
both cling but know that the change must be killed.

Escape (No One Said the Coming Dystopia Would Be So Tedious)

Return to form for the Times Square landscape.
Still, it's a shock we didn't get back there
before these recent news reports of rape
and grand and petty larcenies, bugbears
not-so fantastical, and mundane scrapes
pushed back in mind the eighties' Gotham scares.

Some picture heroes rushing in to save
us from ourselves or just to blow it all
to pieces. Vibrant cities turn to graves
of crime, dropped commerce, all else that appalls . . .
and still the apathetic deem to stave
off this decline by winking at the sprawl.

Not fleeing is what's frankly cowardly
if we shield eyes in acts of worried pleas.

John Self(less)

for Martin Amis (1949–2023)

"How goes the agitators of the world,
as I, like most of us, indulge, awaiting
oblivion? You call it vice while curled
asleep with books, but it must be so grating
to you as I gorge life by not relating
to scantiness you desire for me, but I'm
the truly martyred one by wading my slime
through all five boroughs of this guignol city
as well as London-by-the-Thames teatimes
that hide a loud song of salacity."

Your '81 passed years ago,
lit tastes will shift, and Larkin, Bellow,
and Hitchens are dead and gone to mellow.
Blackout the ending of your show.

The Prophet's Voice (In Memoriam Dave Smith, 1950–2022)

The future called, and you replied with recalled sounds,
those stored in polysynth design with quick renown.

Six-thousand units sold. In numbers, seems a meager
amount, but sundry artists heard, and were so eager

to tease the coming new wave age with synthesis,
the last of analog, before the digital bliss

few say that we now live. Not perfect, but revised
for every tech development, it advertised

that eighties life was here to stay, though perhaps, change
in little declines as from that time we're estranged.

It isn't that surprising Carpenteresque tones
returned in times of social media and drones.

We seek solace in memory of simpler times,
which even if it wasn't simple, felt sublime.

How oscillator and microprocessor chips
affect more generations with learned craftsmanship!

"Let's Go," and "Drive," among the cinematic scores
of Tangerine Dream, sequenced moves took on dancefloors

across the neon-stained nightclubs, and still the young
embraced this middle-aged mood as prophetic song.

Portals

Come walk between the aisles and see what's new
upon the shelves, but there's just floating faces,
a harbinger that something's gone askew,

but you still ask if what I say is true,
and I reply to you with lessened grace,
"Just walk among the films and see what's new."

And though we're full since we left the drive-thru,
emptiness shrouds the gut as fingers trace
the "poster art" of something gone askew.

Is this small thing something to ballyhoo
as others crowd around us in this place,
then shift around the shelves to see what's new?

It's not that I want you to misconstrue
that I won't buy some disc despite distaste
for covers that just sit the shelf askew,

but I beg others have some point-of-view
about these artless hosts of floating faces,
but they just walk away to see what's new
among these mirrors of art gone askew.

Silver Screen Maestro

Life would be easier if music played
as leitmotifs among our friends and strangers
we come across at random. It would aid
what we should feel at the right time. The dangers
invisible would be revealed, charades
of what was truly felt would drop, and anger,
embarrassment, and yearning would not be
ashamed of. Life would take reality

and make it something more, and this is what
he does each time a soundtrack or a theme
is scored. Who knew that symphonies still crushed
through skin to bones of those used to extremes
in lyricalness? Not that tears would gush
from eyes, but as you gazed up to the stream
of stars, there would be something glistening there.
Your mood's with this neo-romantic heir

though some called him a thief for they had heard
something about Erich Korngold's *King's Row,*
Star Wars, and *Superman,* and that he'd blurred
the themes together, hoping none would know.
Then add some of Stravinsky's *The Firebird*
as well, but it's just strings across the bows,
the brass and drums expressing mirrored visions
of Gustav with imperial precision.

Stravinsky lived this fact: "Great artists steal."
Not that they take things note by note, but they
use what was good or worse and then conceal
it under themes or melodies that play
for a new age. It's fitting that appeal
to Spielberg's cultural age would outweigh
the worn-out Schoenberg trend that mystifies
and for the wrong cause makes the public cry.

McDonald's and Me

It might mean something that the '82
children's film meant little growing up.
Spielberg was great, but a cheap fraud in lieu
of whimsical wonder clipped my ticket stub.

It's '88: Let's trash the Reese's Pieces
and wipe away our sentimental tears.
A new friend haunts the screen through his caprices
that invite us to hug Ronald sans fear.

Years later, there's still sentiment for Coke
and Skittles and Big Macs despite much of
it tasting now as off or worse. Life's joke
that what we prize in youth will ebb in love,
but movie scores can prick and bring the feels
we lost though the flicks are not so ideal.

Small-Town Lights

Internal pressures push him out the door,
and while thoughts aren't fixed to why he'll go, he's sure.
He heads downtown to where remains some action
despite the time of night. Lights drive the passion:

the windows down, the sounds of pulsed synthwave
takes on the humid air, and all but save
his latest disappointment energizes,
for even the small-town man fantasizes,

and though he keeps mute as his mind implores
when grasping at the neon signs he's fashioned
as myths of variegated lives that he craves,
harsh evidence they're low too, brutalizes.

The Bookstore Jazz Quartet

Across the table conversation spreads
as fierce wildfires withholding nothing in
intensity, and savage words are said,
shooting out their mouths as aural sins.

He drops a point, but rebuttals are next raised—
the loud debates concerning policies
disapproved while seeking the perfect phrase
to fuel contention for the cause of peace.

As voices climb past to the spires of books
clustered around the sterile dueling match,
strolling patrons bash the table with looks
so sharp and measured that a cautious slatch

blows throughout the nervous atmosphere,
and the four leave again, hushing the scene
to the wan quiet of a funeral bier,
where patrons yield to tame their growing spleen.

The Day Death Walked into a Restaurant

He walked through the door smelling like hot piss,
a scent that shot as high as it could rise,
saturating the store with rottenness.
Thus, it's a wonder he didn't draw in flies

to the establishment. Disturbing staff,
he leaned over the counter, sifting smells
so harsh that one should engrave an epitaph,
for it reeked as if Death came into dwell.

Certainly, a colostomy pouch gripped
his ribs, providing escape for his trapped waste.
It's good the staff hushed, halting unkind slipped
remarks. The only wish was for his haste

outdoors after he'd been served. It's such a shame
that they all felt this way, but what if some
other patrons walked in? None could they blame
but the old man they wished had never come.

Nagel Ladies

Chromatic models pop from every page,
entice with Deco smiles while coal-black hair
and voguish bleach-white skin are posed, assuage
his appetite for something debonair.

It's wild that man can turn the drawn 2D
to visualized 3D as angles shaped
to bounding curves that settle down as draped,
transforming print into reality.

Hollywood's Last Cowboy

Sincerity was always negligible,
    with the past golden years of Tinseltown
    praised being no exception. There were clowns
drunk on group faddish thought and rigmarole
    concerning some cause said in evening gowns.

Banality as fashion has grown worse.
    Cliched reiterating: "Never meet
    your heroes," or you'll soon perceive deceit
beneath the winning smiles, and what's perverse
    revealed on the web as their agents tweet.

But he avoided the childhood pitfalls
    encasing even those beholden to
    the Mouse, and those remaining sane are few
among new Hollywood. Career baseball
    to *Elvis,* then to his *Escape* breakthrough.

Decades have passed, and physically he's changed
    from action star to a supporting player,
    but navigating the news, no naysayers
have spoken lasting words as charm has ranged
    across all kinds, disclosing fandom's layers.

Adventure Remains

Swashbuckler, rogue, and hero hesitant
        sometimes, become the power of playtime
where we remember scenes and don't supplant
        with louder action-packed fare. At bedtime
we fell asleep to read-along cassettes
as stories played through and then were reset.

Back when you had a smirk, the feeling still
        had charm that fluttered women's hearts, and made
their husbands proud as men again, while thrills
        enraptured beaming children as they swayed
from side to side in seats. See what a joy
it was to have such effects but not cloy!

But you've changed now, and still I don't blame you
        as much as I could try. It's likely not
your fault that the good roles have become few
        or that the good roles rest in wretched plots.
There's comfort knowing that the blaster, whip,
fedora, and much more remains as hip.

Avian Equation

This space-time presented as such
        is y, the results of plus x.
And what is x? The whining crows
across clipped grass who bring a touch
        of gloaming back and interject

a solemn mood into a pared
        down green. Then two plump doves stretch, twitch
their bobbing heads to make pained coos
as the crows rush their turn as cared-
        for sneaks, and yet their stuttered fits

are nothing but exposed design,
        for crows hounding fat doves express
what y is. Y is the push-pull
between the two forces, and lines
        scraped on the broken grass profess

the give-and-take dueling observed.
        Without x, y would be as null
as cooing sputtered to some void,
but paired, the crows' and doves' trilled verve
        melds, settling down as something droll.

The Byrd (Annus Horribilis)

They've just announced, "We're shutting down The Byrd,"
the news proclaims, "They're soon closing The Byrd,"
and as we watch reports, it's what we feared.

Recalled some months before viewing *The Thing,*
and now some months later viewing these things,
I'm not too scared but ponder life's downswing.

It's weird that recently the seats were crowded,
and strange in memory that lines were crowded,
but we remember past emotions shouted,

when theaters would play the movies seen,
and theaters like this were Friday's scene,
where mustered patrons merged to seek what's screened.

The Wurlitzer would play to hail the night,
the organ player banged the keys that night
until the curtains pulled back. Daylight

has ended at the right time so the film . . .
has ended at the right time so the film
can set a proper mood. Would I be thrilled?

But all of that is just a memory,
and what was seen becomes just memories,
but as I stop, I'll hail The Byrd's marquee,

for one day it'll open like before,
and that one day I'll be there as before
as jubilation pairs with open doors!

*** (after re-opening)

Though entrants are still wary, it's rebirth,
though fear remains this new year, it's rebirth,
and despite disappointments, there's some mirth.

Video Armageddon

There were some days a pocketful of quarters
made one feel rich, as when wise Solomon
received the Sheban Queen and kingdom borders
were crossed beneath a dry Near Eastern sun.
With our hands full, we rushed the cramped arcade
and made it our domain. The lingering smoke
would drift around the room. We weren't afraid
of older teens and what our wins provoked.
At homes we gamed as long. From memory,
up, up, down, down, left, right, left, right, b, a,
select, plus *Super Mario Bros. 3*
awed us despite how many times we played,
but what would thrill us more is Christ as head
of his vanguard, sword pointed, but no dread.

Not So Similar

"Are we the same?" This thought, which cramped my brain
and guts, I brooded on after she wrote
blunt words as hooks, revealing covert disdain
for collegiate learning her peers said by rote.
She thinks the messy paths of history
are subject to interpretation, time
leaves stains like gunshots in the mysteries
and noirs she loves, and strange thoughts taste sublime.

How I desired that I had learned to play
piano as a little boy. I'm jealous
a little of the talent you possess,
but know the more distinctions you display
will aid to being closer, so I'll relish
you as the greater shadow, my pride's test.

Home Sweet Home

Such effort for a little one,
      my conscience cheered your will,
and I let your spinning alone
      to duck as the web feels
as I expected, but my sprinting
      beyond still had me startled.
As evening folded and last glinting
      light on your kingdom hurtled
my body past, I realized
      that home is relative,
that comfort, symmetry, and size
      make varied ways to live
for humans, insects, and arachnids.
      Goodwill halted. The web
drew up a second time this placid
      wee interloper's dread,
and failed both predator and prey,
      not for want of their skills,
but because rushing fear outplayed
      what fanged survival willed.

Florida Fire Ant Tide

Beyond the recessed ground and flooded farm
they journey north, away from the storm's dross
that washed away their queen as garbage tossed
across the floating chaff. En masse they swarm
as pain personified, the cyclone's scythe
that reaps a harvest against fleeing pets
and owners. Swimming down the flush, they whet
the bellies' sting against the flotsam, blithe
to what's behind though they've lost many soldiers
along the path since the storm dropped. The march
continues with form shifting ovate to arch
as people convey askance at the sojourn
discharged from the marshlands, which used to parch
at summer's peak, now shrouding drenched exposure.

Crocodiles and Tigers

*It is the inalienable right of every man,
woman, and child to wear khaki.*
   —The Official Preppy Handbook

Proud crocodiles and tigers on the prowl
        head to the beach, pacing to beat the stir
of early crowds with heads held high, their towels
        draped over shoulders, and game mused as sure.

Bold crocodiles and tigers spring their hunt
        for what appeals to their swift eyes, the barest
of flesh that poses and struts oceanfront
        boardwalks: the darkened, the browned, and the fairest.

These leering crocodiles and tigers weigh
        their choice and stride away from the boardwalk,
but while they chase, there's nothing to allay
        lured carnivores who sniff the crowded dock.

And if these crocodiles and tigers schmooze
        their prey aboard moored yachts, what then? The chase
returns as they pop collars, down their booze,
        begin their practiced chats, then play straight-faced.

Sly crocodiles and tigers slip their smiles
        amidst sophomoric scenes aped on the sea,
and yet these hunts will go on as cheap wiles
        of cads tempt targets—this they'll guarantee.

James County Mall Memorial

The malls are getting more and more crowded.
Customers will come online and find an easy place to shop.
—Robert J. Fisher

When I was young, I should've known your tricks:
You claimed to be a place that dispensed dreams.
Those were the precious days we thought would last,
before rough cynicism dropped to memes.
Where were the arcades, greasy fast-food stands
and other magnets? Always fraudulence
wasn't it? Yes, I should've known what's real,
was not to be, but where's the recompense?
Now driving by piled bricks, what comes to mind
are teenage times—a new high school was built
across the street a few years back, and then,
the police station: see memories guilt
for what was, could've been, but I still smile
though sounds of toppled stores blast the landscape.
And those of falling dispositions stand
still while their moods engage plans for escape.
Back then the wanting guise of this dead mall
still purposed much for shoppers floating store
to store, some hand in hand, or even those
alone withdrawn on that wide single floor.
Disgrace to other malls, (I traveled south
to Patrick Henry and Coliseum Malls
before the downturn overcame), you were
of the community despite the faults,
and as a part, but now no more, some praise
is due despite frustration built across
the three decades you opened your blue doors
as you're remade to concrete and our loss.

Popcorn

He tosses kernels up to catch
with either hand or mouth,
and lets chance drop them anywhere
they'll fall among the crowd.
Imagination goes pop-pop tonight

Some group of laughing teens let fly
the kernels from their fingers
to pelt obtrusive couples kissing,
their taste of loving lingers.
Imagination goes pop-pop tonight

But others shuffle near the seats,
avoiding being tripped
by stretching legs while their shoes crunch
the viscid floor. None slipped.
Imagination goes pop-pop tonight

And once the film has ended, bags
are ditched into the piling
receptacles that bury these
remains that bought their smiling.
Imagination goes pop-pop tonight

So be it buttered, salted, plain,
or more, accessory
to evening-ritual screen events,
enrich the films they see!
Imagination goes pop-pop tonight

II. Iconoclasts

Iconoclast

Fires manufactured devastates the fleet
encroaching from the south. Its elements
a mystery. From God's mouth roils a heat
that curdles blood with ash's spun ascent.

Such holy flames are great, especially
within the halting conscience, exciting men
with agitation to push forward sprees
against their idols and repent their sins.

The excommunicated mock pale threats
from Rome. The pope's authority is null.
Thus, Leo smashes all with no regrets
when comes against his name the papal bull.

Are all these intrigues killed as by Greek fire
as life continues under now-dimmed spires?

Valens' Dreams at Adrianople

What is the nature of Rome? Place or culture?
Would the sun set on this city as change
occurs, never noticed but by the vultures
of history? My Eastern city strange!

Christ's nature is up for debate so preached
Nicomedia and Lucian, priests
of controversial doctrines. Men sing each
to their own faith, aware of tales from beasts.

These Balkan landscapes, host to centuries
of war, do bleed our conscience. What dull dreams
were killed on the fields of Edirne? Pleas
delineate Byzantine-born sense and schemes.

Speak, last true Roman, though no Roman son,
the horse becomes the tank, the sword the gun.

Old Devil

If you can't annoy somebody, there's little point in writing.
                                        —Kingsley Amis

Most artists encourage themselves as ones
athwart the powers placed at chance, enthroned
to punch up as they claim to be most grown
in judgement while declaring what is fun
and morally correct, and smile to shun
those whose wrong thoughts have earned them the first stones
propelled at them, but right thoughts are just cloned
from the same powers from whom they take funds.
Though three decades have passed since he has died,
the more that one fat Englishman becomes
again as relevant and poignant when
a modern controversy roils those in
good grace, for he enjoyed a cultural scrum
against the literary mandarins' pens
and stressed his loves—pop culture and mixed gins.

Bright Light, Some City (After Edward Hopper's *Morning Sun*)

*It's probably a reflection of my own, if I may say, loneliness.
I don't know. It could be the whole human condition.*
—Edward Hopper

Why does it matter that the sun has seemed
to seek her out as she awakes above
the morning rush that pushes out slipped dreams
that fog her rising while there's still no love?

Now looking out the glass, she wonders if
those outside feel the same, despite if they
arose as two: their bodies, sheets, and breath
together though they live like shadow plays.

And still within a crowd the sentiments
won't differ much amongst the shifting mass,
and she, above it all, tries making sense
of what a good life is, and then it flashed—

She thinks, "I should be satisfied the rays
still warm this aging body, that the view
provides a worn delight, and I can pray
that pain will pass, as will these cresting blues."

But will it pass despite a wish to chance
for more from now? She wills to force a change
of personality as her eyes glance
beyond the noise that makes her life mundane.

"No matter what's before me, I'm enriched
by my imaginative lambency,
accustomed to the urban droning pitch
that ripples softly in this towered sea."

For mourning should not be confused with morning,
she settles her pink nightgown on the sheet
and leans ahead to paint a world with yearning
that someone might feel like her on the street.

To the Nation's Credit

Before he sought the presidential spot
three times, (a losing gesture manifest
in all accounts), he railed against the plots
of slavocracy that had driven the test
of the states, if they should remain. His brother,
at one point pushed to madness, (what newsmen
had said), knew that men made to rise must suffer
the meting out that cause most to give in.

His friend Fred Douglass knew that service must
be handled with responsibility.
Dear God, not Mr. Blaine! This antitrust
legislation . . . the public voice agrees.

Brief letters sent then helped to face the hushed
retirement as he sat dull dinners and teas.

Indian Hill Cemetery, 1953

True Cincinnati spirit is the love
of hearth, the principles of isolation,
a life in works of service to the nation.
Could he reverse the course, release the doves
of peace, he'd throw his barbs at what he felt
were dangers to the American way of life,
decrying Roosevelt's class war as strife
not fit for the hearty sons of the steel belt,
and raised his voice, protesting the decade
growth of regulation halting men
from their potential liberty, with a grin
that said that the fed budget must be paid.

In chambers of the Senate a brusque voice
is quelled as Eisenhower becomes the choice.

George Schuyler and the *Pittsburgh Courier,* 1964

"Honored sir, we recognize your service
at the *Pittsburgh Courier* these past years.
Your latest words have made us very nervous,
although we used to love your wit that pierced

that worthy of contempt, your tongue has steeled
too far this time: You shouldn't disrespect
Dr. Martin Luther King's ideals
with all your talk about how he infects

the United States as a typhoidal strain.
We know you've talents no other column writer
since Mencken had to shift against the grain,
but you've become to us an ill-timed griper."

His hope for social strife was mixing up,
. . . as a white ewe by a black ram is tupped.

Power Battle

They could have done it better with an axe.
—George Westinghouse

God said, "Let There Be Light and There Was Light,"
then Westinghouse threw down his challenge in
response to Edison's designs. "This fight
against my currents won't ease your chagrin.
Such sloppiness, inventor! Menlo Park
should've been proud to have such a "smart man,"
but you've become a scoundrel, such a stark
divide from your outward persona, hands
applauding for that stunt with the convict
Kemmler. Oh yes, the law rewarded him.
The flesh surged through with light, made derelict
by smear campaigns. See how lows come from wins!"

The energies that serve this war are sparks
that wouldn't aid sly Tom's electric plans.

Culture Warrior

There is no better motto which it [culture] can have than these words of Bishop Wilson, "To make reason and the will of God prevail."
—Matthew Arnold

Cerebral verse has fled the mind, withdrawn
as Thyrsis left without saying goodbye,
his presence felt beyond the Oxford lawn
and heard on autumn winds as plangent sighs.

New work proclaimed as balderdash is shelved
as fancy of a man who has lost touch
with tough prudential words. His mind he helved
for prose, while verse he had laid in his hutch.

It fell away as his beleaguered faith
trembled before the rushing tide of doubts,
that terrifying banshee wail which wraiths
in Celtic tales would sputter forth to rout.

As Crassus of the Triumvirate was,
it's shameful that Matt Arnold has no buzz.

Life Turns Tragic for Mr. Charles Beaumont

Wasting away like Walter Jameson,
the faculties depart down the hourglass.
Poor end for *The Twilight Zone's* famous son:
only death could break this cruel impasse.
Reality unfolds from science fiction.
Beware! the shadows overstretch the brain:
Time flits away it all: the plots, the diction,
the commentary, excised without pain.
This macabre scene is such a poignant haunting
for other writers. Write now, write well! death
could be around the corner, leaving wanting
your legacy with wheezing swallowed breaths.
Go waste away dark star below weird plane
existence that could make the sane insane.

How the Stars Flicker Under Eyes (Cowboy Strode)

L.A. or Spain, the desert is the same
despite distance across the Atlantic Ocean.
When eyes of voyeurs penetrate, you tame
your tongue, lather your sun-torched legs with lotion,
and as sweat drips like tears into stone eyes,
you turn, stare back, and wink a knowing wink
at the film camera lens. You realize
surmise is that something people will drink
up without much reflection on the status
quo. Here is a man, brown as swallowed dirt
in swollen lungs, and the lens, his afflatus
for swallowing down the sun-scorched land that hurts.

Here sweats the man who pushed friendship in gratis—
For it's his eyes, not words, that truth imparts.

Mr. Montgomery, Keep Movin'

Y'all hear those arpeggios swing high?
I know when sprinting arpeggios swing high,
he's sounding out those trembling licks like sighs.

A Hoosier son and a man with talented hands,
Midwestern son and man with machinist hands,
you broke in your corn with Lionel Hampton's band.

You shook your fist at the jazz purists' complaints
and threw your nonchalance at critics' complaints.
How could they understand what pop tunes paint?

The hard bop sound, though cool, makes a man poor,
that tired bop sound, though funky, makes a man poor,
but those critics never worked sores on old sores.

I guess what y'all hear is a falling chord
letting loose the strokes across the fretboard.

Eyes Open

Stand up for your rights and be brave, and don't be intimidated. Read your Bible. That's really given me strength, and it will give you strength. Pray, and use God's name, Jehovah. And never tell a lie, ever.
—Margaret Keane

Black orbs that peer out from the canvas paint
meet estranged eyes that pant for each detail.
The mystery within the silent, faint
image remains as the colors outside pale.

Bold eyes that seek drawn dreams, where do you search
now that your higher revelation calls?
Do those eyes dazzle as a crackling torch
before a flagging cavern-hunter's lull?

Her painted children creep out from the oil
in tears, then laughing as real children act,
their stares lined up with your stares, eyes bugged out,
and circling these black voids like brilliant coils,
resplendent atmospheric prisms track
the brushed down lines to faith from bitter doubts.

Longstreet's Postbellum Letters

"Bob Lee, you should've gone round to the right,
outflanking them that fearsome second day
as then I saw depart from those eyes light
that flickered when came back the wounded gray,
withdrawing from the charge that cracked the south's
last hope. I knew your stolid heart was bound
with honor for the fallen men. Proud mouths
now closed, the rested were interred in grounds
too many miles from southern soil. Good sir,
I'm still "Old Pete," your warhorse at command.
Why do they speak as if I lost the war
when only in thought did I countermand
those orders given? 'Cause I sprung my plans
for fostering the brotherhood of man?"

Red Warren's Red Loam

What secrets pass within the briar patch?
The shameful pride of histories reflects
across the Tennessee farmyard where hatch
the fruitage of young life spring resurrects.

Cold shovels dig beneath the packed red loam,
red hair over red dirt; is it the other
way around? Go brood as the hearthstone
is scuffed by feet, you semi-blind star-lover.

Books say that minds never go home again,
our current sentiments divide us from
what we once thought, those buried childhood fears.
You stare into your gnarled and aged-stained hands
and pull from entrails a curse for the downed sun
while telescoping oscillating spheres.

The Last Roman of the South (Allen Tate)

Conserving the traditions of the past,
Kentucky son, with your neo-classical verse
and molding your personality in casts
of marble forms, you pictured the mortal hearse
of Greco-Roman antiquity astride
the twentieth century roadway and spilled
tears over Aeneas as he sails the tides
searching for a new homeland to be tilled.
As a young man you rebuked Mr. Hughes,
declaiming that "maybe in the North they might
meet as equal artists," but then saw a bright
future for Ellison and reshaped your views
concerning the societal questions that remained
while you held firm to your classical quatrains.

Hear the *Kaiju* Roar (Akira Ifukube)

If the beat marches, let it march as grand
movements across the broken landscape. Tone
can be as bountiful *hayate* blown
against the jagged coastline. Marching band,
call forth the images of *Kaiju* film,
the men and monsters, metaphors of some
calamity I barely know. At helm
is music in our childhood we could hum
out of tune, as across the T.V. screen
fake monsters met actors in bloodless wars.
Even those who can't read music know the score,
it's all the same, the final act and scene,
the leather glove across the double bass.

Could you recall a safer childhood place?

Pop Pulp (Spillane)

The bullets from the .45 have patterns
as they scream for their targets, human marks
for smoking guns. This evening busty slatterns
are cracked over the head, and gangsters park
their cars behind abandoned buildings. True,
the clichéd themes abound. But O what fire
is that hard, gritty prose! Prose where the blues
twang softly with background of squealing tires.
Rat-a-tat-tat, typewriting as gunshots
across the page delivers thrills to wives
and schoolboys: Tens of million copies bought,
a legacy from which Frank Miller thrives.
      Divorce from self the falsities, the caught
      hardboiled truth has deep power, and does it drive!

Sundown at Kenyon College

Bent down, he searches for names lost
among the plotted, weathered stones,
these tablets probing distant thoughts
when crouched above some poet's bones.

Then there's some noise at the site's edge,
and eyes aroused, he notices
three huddled students laugh and tread
the graveyard with betraying bliss.

He thinks some sacrilege should be
declared for this cool nonchalance,
but then reflects, "If Crowe could see,
he'd say, 'They know the meter's dance.'"

And heading to the parking lot,
though not as glum, something's not right
he reckons as he views the plot,
but no more time, there's little light.

Notes

"Wave Cycles": *Out Run* is a 1986 Sega arcade driving game. Simmons (Richard) is a popular exercise guru. Voight-Kampff is a test to discern replicants (androids) in the novel *Do Androids Dream of Electric Sleep?* and its film adaptation *Blade Runner*. Star Wars was used as a pejorative for the proposed Strategic Defense Initiative in the 1980s.

"Questing the Imagination": The Ark of the Covenant of Biblical and *Raiders of the Lost Ark* fame.

"Sidekicks and Dames": Short Round was portrayed by the actor Ke Huy Quan in *Indiana Jones and the Temple of Doom*.

"History's Wild Dance (Re-Reading *Blood Meridian*)": The Brileys were a notorious set of brothers who terrorized Richmond, VA in 1979. They executed a notorious prison break in 1984. Seth is the third son of Adam.

"Second Inauguration": This poem references the 1985 North American cold wave. The Gipper is President Ronald Reagan; see film *Knute Rockne, All American*.

"Back to Reality after Space-Time Conundrums": McFly of *Back to the Future*.

"More Android Than Androids": Nexus-Six is a replicant model in *Blade Runner*.

"Mutating Passion": For Titus Andronicus, see *Titus Andronicus*, Act III, Scene 2.

"Escape (No One Said the Coming Dystopia Would Be So Tedious)": Statistically, 1981 is the most violent year in NYC history.

"John Self(less)": John Self is the protagonist of the 1984 novel *Money*.

"The Prophet's Voice (In Memoriam Dave Smith, 1950–2022)": Dave Smith created the Prophet-5 synthesizer, which revolutionized sound design and scoring, particularly in genre films.

"Silver Screen Maestro": Erich Korngold composed the score for the film *Kings Row*. Stravinsky was a composer of Modernism. "Gustav" is Gustav Mahler, the Late Romantic composer. Schoenberg was a composer of the Second Viennese School.

"McDonald's and Me": The '82 children's film is, of course, *E.T.*

"Hollywood's Last Cowboy": The Mouse references Disney.

"The Byrd (Annus Horribilis)": Wurlitzer is a famous, now defunct, brand of instruments.

"Video Armageddon": For Sheban Queen, see 1 Kings 1:10. *Super Mario Bros. 3* is one of the most popular NES titles.

"James County Mall Memorial": Patrick Henry Mall is in Newport News, VA. The now demolished Coliseum Mall was in Hampton, VA.

"Iconoclast": Byzantine Iconoclasm began during Leo III the Isaurian's reign.

"Valens' Dreams at Adrianople": Emperor Valens was an adherent of Arian Christianity as were his Gothic opponents. Nicomedia references Eusebius, who, along with Lucian, was as well.

"Bright Light, Some City (After Edward Hopper's *Morning Sun*)": The title is a twist on the 1984 novel *Bright Lights, Big City.*

"To the Nation's Credit": His brother is William T. Sherman. James G. Blaine was a towering figure in the second half of 19th-century politics. Due to the controversy over the Mulligan letters, his reputation suffered.

"Indian Hill Cemetery, 1953": Cincinnati has been the home base for the Taft political dynasty.

"George Schuyler and the *Pittsburgh Courier,* 1964": The *Pittsburgh Courier* (1907–1966) was a leading black newspaper. For tupped, see *Othello,* Act I, Scene I.

"Power Battle": William Francis Kemmler was the first person to be executed by the electric chair.

"Culture Warrior": Refers to the First Triumvirate of Caesar, Pompey, and Crassus. Matthew Arnold doesn't have a legacy as compared with Alfred Tennyson and Robert Browning.

"Life Turns Tragic for Mr. Charles Beaumont": Due to Beaumont's early death, "Long Live Walter Jameson" was an ironic story for him to have written.

"Longstreet's Postbellum Letters": During Reconstruction, Longstreet led black troops against the anti-Reconstruction White League during the Battle of Canal St. in New Orleans.

"The Last Roman of the South (Allen Tate)": Langston Hughes and Ralph Ellison

"Hear the *Kaiju* Roar (Akira Ifukube)": *Kaiju* translates to strange beast, but usually refers to giant monsters. *Hayate* means sudden sound of wind or hurricane.

"Pop Pulp (Spillane)": Frank Miller is a writer for graphic novels such as *The Dark Knight Returns* and *Batman: Year One.*

About the Author

Christopher Fried (1985–) lives in Richmond, VA and works as an ocean shipping logistics analyst. His poetry collection, *All Aboard the Timesphere,* was published in 2013 by Kelsay Books. His National Indie Excellence award-winning novel, *Whole Lot of Hullabaloo: A Twenty-First Century Campus Phantasmagoria,* was published in 2020. He was an advisor on the 1980s science fiction film documentary *In Search of Tomorrow* (2022).

www.ingramcontent.com/pod-product-compliance
Lightning Source LLC
Chambersburg PA
CBHW031200160426
43193CB00008B/458